HOW TO MULCH

Save Water, Feed the Soil, and Suppress Weeds

Stu Campbell and Jennifer Kujawski

DELPHI PUBLIC LIBRARY

222 East Main Street
Delphi, Indiana 46923
765-564-2929

*The mission of Storey Publishing is to serve our customers by
publishing practical information that encourages
personal independence in harmony with the environment.*

Edited by Carleen Madigan
Series design by Alethea Morrison
Art direction by Jeff Stiefel
Text production by Theresa Wiscovitch
Indexed by Christine R. Lindemer, Boston Road Communications

Cover and interior illustrations by © Steve Sanford

© 1991, 2001, 2015 by Storey Publishing
A previous edition of this book was published under the title *Mulch It!* The
text has been completely revised and updated by Jennifer Kujawski for this
edition.

All rights reserved. No part of this book may be reproduced without written permission from the publisher, except by a reviewer who may quote brief passages or reproduce
illustrations in a review with appropriate credits; nor may any part of this book be
reproduced, stored in a retrieval system, or transmitted in any form or by any means —
electronic, mechanical, photocopying, recording, or other — without written permission
from the publisher.
    The information in this book is true and complete to the best of our knowledge.
All recommendations are made without guarantee on the part of the author or Storey
Publishing. The author and publisher disclaim any liability in connection with the use of
this information.
    Storey books are available for special premium and promotional uses and for custom-
ized editions. For further information, please call 1-800-793-9396.

Storey Publishing
210 MASS MoCA Way
North Adams, MA 01247
www.storey.com

Printed in the United States by McNaughton & Gunn, Inc.
10 9 8 7 6 5 4 3 2 1

LIBRARY OF CONGRESS CATALOGING-IN-PUBLICATION DATA

Campbell, Stu.
  How to mulch : save water, feed the soil, and suppress weeds / Stu Campbell and
  Jennifer Kujawski.
      pages cm. — (Storey basics)
  Includes index.
  ISBN 978-1-61212-444-5 (pbk. : alk. paper)
  ISBN 978-1-61212-445-2 (ebook) 1. Mulching. I. Title. II. Series: Storey basics.
S661.5.C34 2015
635'.04—dc23
                        2014029013

CONTENTS

PART ONE

THE WHYS AND WHATS OF MULCHING

Once thought of primarily for vegetable gardens, mulch has come a long way. It's now recognized as an essential ingredient for more beautiful and easier-to-maintain flower beds and landscape plantings of all kinds. And mulch has many important environmental benefits as well, one of the most important of which is water conservation.

Many kinds of materials can be used for mulching. The mulch materials you choose for your vegetable garden can be practical but not necessarily beautiful. On the other hand, you'll find dozens of mulching choices for use around your landscape plantings and flower beds, where the mulch itself can be an important feature of the overall design.

There is no one "right" way to mulch. There are good ways, and there are not-so-good ways. In addition to providing solutions to common mulching concerns, this book offers suggestions about ways to mulch your gardens to make them happier, healthier, and more rewarding.

MANY REASONS TO MULCH. A neatly mulched garden can bring many rewards.

THE BENEFITS OF MULCHING

FROM IMPROVING SOIL to suppressing weeds, mulching brings many benefits to your gardens and landscaped areas. You will also be able to walk around in your garden on rainy days and not have 3 inches of mud stuck to the soles of your shoes. The following list covers mulching's essential benefits.

Mulch Retains Moisture

Mulch's ability to conserve soil moisture has long been documented (up to 50 percent in some studies). This water-conserving value can't be overemphasized, especially during times of water restrictions, shortages, and drought conditions.

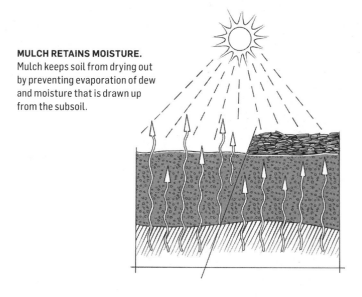

MULCH RETAINS MOISTURE.
Mulch keeps soil from drying out by preventing evaporation of dew and moisture that is drawn up from the subsoil.

Mulch helps prevent water in the soil from evaporating. Some impervious mulches, such as black plastic, do not allow air or water to pass into or out of the soil. Permeability is something to keep in mind when selecting a type of mulch (see How to Choose a Mulch, page 43).

Mulch Suppresses Weeds

Mulching can practically eliminate the need for weeding and cultivating. There are a few catches, however.

First, the mulch itself must be weed free. If it is not, you will end up introducing a whole new pesky crop of weeds.

Second, mulch must be deep enough to prevent existing weed seeds from taking root. Weed seedlings need light to grow. If mulch is applied too thinly, weeds may be able to poke through.

Finally, mulches won't smother all weeds. Some particularly hearty weeds have the fortitude to push through just about any barrier. In a well-mulched bed, though, these intruders should be easy to spot and even more easily plucked.

If the mulch is deep, weed seedlings that sprout in darkness will wither away.

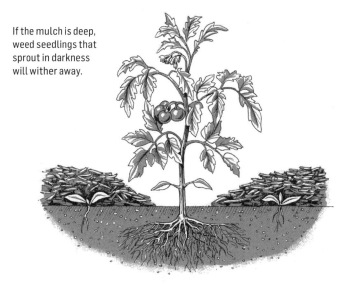

If the mulch is too thin, some weeds will poke through. Even then, they are easy to spot and easy to pull.

Mulch Insulates from Heat and Cold

Simply stated, mulch is insulation. It can keep the soil around your plants' roots cooler during hot days and warmer during cool nights.

In winter, mulch works to prevent soil from rapidly freezing and thawing and so prevents the soil from heaving, which causes root damage to your plants. Although mulch may not prevent the soil from freezing, it can prevent freezing from happening overnight. It's best to apply winter mulch in late fall, after the ground has frozen. Come spring's warm weather, removing the mulch allows plants to start sprouting new growth.

Mulch also is useful for controlling soil temperatures in summer. Applied in the spring after the soil starts to warm up, mulch should remain in place for the majority of the growing season. Extremely high soil temperatures can hinder root growth and damage some shallow-rooted plants. During the long, hot days of summer, mulch can reduce soil temperature by as much as 10°F.

Some plants, such as tomatoes, eggplants, and peppers, thrive in heat. Dark mulches, such as black or red plastic, warm the soil and have been shown to increase fruit yields for plants such as these (see Mulching Vegetables on page 69).

Mulch Controls Erosion and Improves Soil

Mulch absorbs the impact of falling raindrops and, as a result, prevents soil compaction and crusting. Water penetrates through loose, granulated soil but runs off hard, compacted earth. Mulch controls erosion by slowing water runoff and wind speed over soil.

Many organic mulches, such as shredded leaves and bark chips, add organic material to soil as they decompose. This material enhances soil structure, which then leads to all sorts of great things, such as improved air, water, and nutrient movement throughout the soil.

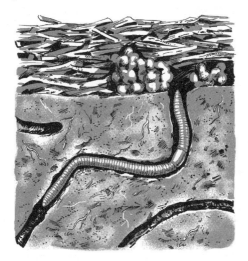

MULCHING SUPPORTS EARTHWORMS. Earthworms create spaces for air and water movement in soil under mulch, and their castings include nutrients from digested mulch.

In addition, mulch encourages earthworms to proliferate. Worms further aerate the soil and release nutrients in the form of their waste, called "castings." Mulch also stimulates increased microbial activity in the soil. Certain bacteria are every bit as important as worms for maintaining healthy soil. Microbes break down organic matter rapidly, which makes nutrients available to plant roots sooner.

Mulch Helps Grow Healthy Plants

Mulched plants are less diseased and more uniform than those without mulch. One reason for this is that mulching prevents fruits, flowers, and other plant parts from being splashed by mud and water. Besides causing unsightly spots and rot, splashing can carry soilborne diseases. Mulch protects ripening vegetables, such as tomatoes, melons, pumpkins, and squash, from direct contact with the soil. That means fewer "bad" spots, rotten places, and mold.

Mulches help control harmful soil nematodes and fungi and can also reduce insect pest populations and some diseases that they spread. Basically, mulching helps reduce plant stress. Healthy, strong plants have the energy and resources to better protect themselves against insects and other pests.

Organic Mulch Increases Soil Nutrients

While not dependable as a primary plant food, organic mulch can contribute nitrogen, potassium, phosphorus, and several trace elements to the soil. The amount of nutrients available from mulch depends on the mulch's age, type, and duration of weathering.

MAKE YOUR OWN MULCH. Convert cut or fallen branches from around the yard into mulch by running them through a chipper.

Mulch Is Environmentally Beneficial

Using mulches for weed control helps reduce your dependence on chemical herbicides. The fewer chemicals you use, the lower the risk of groundwater contamination, general exposure to toxins, and accidental poisonings.

Mulching is an excellent way to reduce and recycle yard waste. Dead plants (that are not diseased or insect-infested), leaves, grass clippings, and old newspapers are fair game for the mulch pile. Even shredded or chopped woody materials can be converted into mulch. However, be sure not to add poison ivy, poison sumac, or poison oak to your mulch.

Mulch Is Attractive

Many people mulch their garden just because they like the way it looks. Mulch makes a garden look a little better or neater. It adds color and texture to the landscape, and covering ornamental beds with shredded bark or hardwood gives a professional touch.

SOME DRAWBACKS TO MULCHING

THERE ARE SOME KEY ISSUES to consider when deciding how to mulch. But with most problems come solutions. Let's look at these considerations one by one.

Controls but Doesn't *Eliminate* Weeds

It's true that mulches can't smother every weed. Robust perennial weeds have been known to push up through straw, wood chips, and black plastic. They've even been known to break through concrete sidewalks!

Solution. Mulching makes it easier to pull out weeds. Remember, mulching is not meant to eliminate all your gardening chores. It simply makes them easier.

May Cause Nitrogen Deficiencies

Any fresh, light-colored, and unweathered organic mulch will "steal" nitrogen from plants during the earliest stages of decomposition. This happens because the microbes breaking down the material use soil nitrogen. Wood-based products, such as sawdust or wood chips, are routinely condemned for doing this, but hay, straw, and leaves also can tie up nitrogen. Eventually, though, these materials will add nutrients back into the soil as they decay.

Solution. To deal with the temporary nitrogen shortage, supplement your garden with additional nitrogen. Try cottonseed meal, alfalfa meal, or a synthetic source such as calcium nitrate or urea.

May Hinder Water Penetration

The case against plastic mulch has always been its inability to let rainwater through to the soil and, ultimately, to the plant roots. The same can be said for some organic types of mulch, such as leaves, if they get matted down.

Solution. If you decide to use plastics, be sure to moisten the ground thoroughly before laying down the material. Place the plastic down and make slits or holes in the vicinity of your plants to allow for watering. Doing so will expose those areas to weed growth, so you may have to pull a couple of stragglers now and then.

As for matted leaves, chopping them beforehand is the best way to prevent matting. For other compacted organic mulches, turn or loosen them occasionally to allow water to reach the soil and plant roots.

LETTING MOISTURE IN. To allow water penetration through plastic mulch, cut slits near plants throughout the material.

Blocks Airflow

Blocking airflow is another shortcoming associated with plastic, but even organic mulches applied too deeply or repeatedly can restrict air movement into the soil. Roots need air to breathe. Many beneficial microorganisms that break down nutrients absorbed by roots also need air to live.

Solution. It's a good practice to get in there and stir things up occasionally. Loosen the crust with a hoe or rake. If you plan on supplementing your mulch because it has lost some of its color and appeal, be careful not to overdo it. There is no need to add 4 inches of mulch when only 1 inch is needed to freshen the appearance.

Provides Breeding Ground for Insects, Slugs, and Snails

You will find an increase in the slug and snail populations when you use mulches, particularly in years with a wet spring. These wet, slimy creatures love the dark, damp areas under a mulch, whether it's organic or black plastic.

Solution. A light dusting of wood ashes, sharp sand, or crushed shells on the ground at the base of plants works well to prevent these pests from feasting on your plants. Slugs and snails don't like to crawl over materials abrasive to their underbellies. These deterrents should be reapplied regularly because they deteriorate with rainfall. Drowning slugs in shallow pans of beer is another option for managing them.

SLUG MANAGEMENT. A shallow pan, such as a pie pan, sunk into the ground and filled with beer works to attract, trap, and drown slugs.

Can Be Unpleasant and Difficult to Handle

Selecting and applying the wrong mulch for your situation can be a big headache. On the other hand, applying an appropriate mulch early in the growing season prevents a lot of problems. For example, a winter mulch application may keep perennials from perishing in the freeze/thaw cycle. If your mulching repertoire is wide enough to allow you to choose the right place for the right mulch at the right time, you can enhance your garden's attractiveness and productivity with a minimum of effort, time, and money.

Solution. If you don't have time or just aren't up to the work of mulching, there are garden care professionals who will gladly deliver and apply mulch to your ornamental beds. For vegetable and small gardens, consider hiring a teenager or local agricultural student to give you a hand. The cost of this help will be minimal compared to the labor of weeding and watering in the summer heat!

May Attract Rodents

Mice and other rodents may take up residence in the warmth and protection of a thick mulch during the cold winter months. As food supplies dwindle, they may elect to gnaw on your favorite fruit tree.

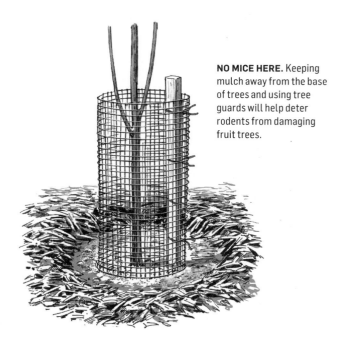

NO MICE HERE. Keeping mulch away from the base of trees and using tree guards will help deter rodents from damaging fruit trees.

Solution. To prevent rodents from feeding on the roots and trunks of your trees or shrubs, never apply an organic mulch all the way up against the base of the plants. Leave 6 to 12 inches of space between the mulch and the tree or shrub. If the mice are going to feed on your tree, they'll have to come out in the cold to do it! You also may want to put a wire shield around the plant base. Quarter-inch hardware cloth works quite well.

May Be a Fire Hazard

Some mulches, such as very dry hay, straw, and sawdust, can catch fire easily.

Solution. Be careful around these mulches. Don't smoke near them, and during extraordinarily dry periods water them occasionally. If you live in an area prone to wildfires, consider using a less flammable mulch, such as stone, in landscape beds.

A FEW DEFINITIONS

HERE SEEMS A GOOD PLACE to explain some terms. These are not meant to be strict, inflexible definitions. They are offered simply as working definitions to describe what is meant when a particular word is used in this book.

Mulch can be any material applied to the soil surface to retain moisture, insulate and stabilize the soil, protect plants, and control weeds. A properly functioning mulch has two basic properties. Good mulch should be (1) light and open enough to permit the passage of water and air and (2) dense enough to inhibit or even choke weed growth.

Mulches can be divided into two fundamental categories:

Organic mulches are like unfinished compost. Anything that will biodegrade (rot) can be used as organic mulch. The most common organic mulches are shredded or chipped bark, leaves and leaf mold, hay, straw, and grass clippings.

Synthetic mulches, sometimes called inert or artificial mulches, don't begin as plant material. They include colored plastics and geotextile landscape fabric, made from polypropylene or polyester.

Here are a few other terms associated with mulching that are sometimes bandied about:

Summer mulches, or growing mulches, are applied in the spring after the soil starts to warm. Throughout the summer they insulate the soil, inhibit weed growth, retain moisture, and control erosion. Both organic and synthetic mulches fall into this category.

Winter mulches are used around woody plants and perennials to insulate against freeze/thaw damage to plants' crowns and roots. Winter mulch is applied in late fall after the soil has cooled, preferably following a hard frost. Winter mulches prevent the soil temperature from jumping up and down, which heaves plants out of the ground. Ordinarily, winter mulches are organic, but geotextiles may provide adequate winter protection.

Living mulches are low-growing, shallow-rooted, ever-spreading ground cover plants such as thyme or pachysandra.

These mulch plants are attractive and commonly used in border flower beds, ornamental plantings, and rock gardens.

Permanent mulches are usually made up of nondisintegrating materials. Permanent mulches such as crushed stone and

USING PERMANENT MULCH. A permanent mulch of stone works well around trees and shrubs.

gravel are useful, particularly in perennial beds, around trees and shrubs, and on soil not likely to be tilled or cultivated.

Green manures, or cover crops, are basically plants like oats, alfalfa, and buckwheat that meet the definition of mulch. They afford fine winter and erosion protection and have the added advantage of attracting beneficial insects during the growing season. They can be either tilled under or harvested and applied as mulch in another part of the garden. Cover crops are used mostly in vegetable gardens or with small fruit plantings.

PART TWO

TYPES OF MULCH

Depending on the material, mulch can be decorative, functional, or both. Biodegradable organic mulches conserve soil moisture and, in varying degrees, add nutrients to the soil. Stones and most inorganic mulches don't improve a soil's health or water retention. Organic and inorganic mulches both largely provide weed and erosion control. Following are descriptions of many common and uncommon mulches.

BARK AND WOOD PRODUCTS

BARK AND WOOD PRODUCTS, scavenged or purchased, have long been used as landscape and garden mulches.

Bark

USES. Decorative and functional.

WHAT IT IS. Bark is probably the most common and versatile of the landscape mulches and comes in a variety of shapes, sizes, colors, and textures. Recommended varieties of bark and wood mulch are listed in Which Wood Is That? on page 25. Bark mulch comes in several sizes (from ¼ inch to 3 inches in diameter) and forms (nuggets, chips, shredded). Bark mulch is sold in bags or in bulk by the cubic yard.

bark nuggets

bark chips

shredded bark mulch

BARK CHOICES. Bark mulch is readily available in several attractive forms, such as nuggets, chips, and shredded.

HOW TO USE IT. Prepare the garden bed, install plants, and water thoroughly and deeply. Then apply mulch like a blanket over the plant's existing or potential roots. Cover the entire bed evenly with a mulch layer 2 to 4 inches thick. Because mulch against a plant stem or tree trunk will invite rot and insects, keep mulch at least 6 inches away from the base of a woody shrub or a tree trunk.

PROS. Readily available in many forms. Attractive. Because it decomposes slowly, bark mulch is less hospitable to artillery fungus (see What's Growing in My Wood Mulch? on page 55).

Evergreen Boughs

USE. Functional.

WHAT THEY ARE. Boughs of conifers are valuable winter protection, especially around newly installed perennials and shrubs; on outdoor containers; and over a bed of spring-flowering bulbs.

HOW TO USE THEM. After the ground is frozen for the winter, lay boughs loosely over garden beds, container plantings, and at the bases of shrubs and small trees. Remove boughs in spring, when sprouts start poking from the ground.

Sawdust

USE. Functional.

WHAT IT IS. The tiny, dustlike wood particles left after wood is sawed.

HOW TO USE IT. Sawdust is frequently recommended as a mulch under blueberries, rhododendrons, and other acid-loving

EVERGREEN MULCH. Lay evergreen boughs over garden plants as a protective winter mulch.

plants. Unweathered pine sawdust decomposes very slowly, so just give it some time to weather and turn gray before you use it. No more than an inch or two of sawdust mulch is needed around most plants.

CONS. Water penetration through sawdust is only fair. Fresh sawdust ties up the nitrogen in a soil (see Some Drawbacks to Mulching, page 11).

Wood Chips

USES. Decorative and functional.

WHAT THEY ARE. Wood chips from a brush chipper generally make excellent mulch. Commercially prepared wood chips are available by the bag and truckload. Colorized wood chips from recycled wood are popular in red, yellow, black, and natural. Some types are chipped, shredded, and dyed red with an environmentally safe coloring to maintain color longer than most natural mulches. Don't confuse this with redwood mulch from trees native to the West Coast.

HOW TO USE THEM. Wood chips are often used on garden paths because they don't tend to become compacted by foot traffic. For your garden apply a 2- to 4-inch layer like a blanket over the soil around your annuals, perennials, and vegetable plants. For trees and shrubs first remove grass and weeds from under the branch canopy. Spread an even layer of wood chips, 2 to 4 inches thick, under the branch spread. Keep chips at least 6 inches away from the plant base.

PROS. Wood chips are economical and commercially available in different hardwood and softwood varieties by bag and bulk. Tree companies in some areas will sometimes offer free excess wood chips from pruning operations.

CONS. Chips don't stay in place as well as barks and may blow or float away. Fresh wood chips temporarily tie up nitrogen during decomposition. Add some nitrogen before planting in soil previously covered with wood chips.

Because wood chips lose their color and decorative appearance much more quickly than bark chips, adding a new layer every year on top of the old can result in overmulching. Over-mulching can choke out shallow-rooted plants and promote disease on susceptible trees and shrubs. To avoid this, rejuvenate your chips every two or three years and add no more than you actually need to create a fresh look.

Which Wood Is That?

Cedar: Bark and/or wood from what is called "red cedar," either juniper or arborvitae

Douglas fir bark: Insect-resistant bark mostly available in the Northwest

Eucalyptus: Ground, shredded hardwood from bark and trunk of sustainably grown trees

Hardwood: Bark and/or wood from deciduous hardwood trees

Hemlock bark: Insect-resistant

Melaleuca: Termite-resistant bark/wood from invasive trees removed from Florida Everglades

Oak bark: Insect-resistant

Pine bark: Widely available by-product of milled pine logs

Redwood bark: Real redwood bark, which is insect-, disease-, and rot-resistant, is from the West Coast. An imitation redwood bark, made of various wood chips dyed red, is widely available.

OTHER PLANT PRODUCTS

MULCHES IN THIS CATEGORY range from ubiquitous — and essentially free — grass clippings and leaves to living ground covers and crops.

Grass Clippings

USE. Functional.

WHAT THEY ARE. Almost anyone with a lawn has grass clippings.

HOW TO USE THEM. Dried clippings are useful as a thinly spread mulch as your first vegetable seedlings come up.

PROS. Besides providing good nutrients, the fine grass will not choke the tiny plants the way that a thicker, coarser mulch might. Overall, grass clippings are good, cheap mulch. They will be already chopped if you use a rotary lawn mower.

CONS. Spread too thickly, clipped grass will make a hot, slimy mess and smell bad. Don't recycle clippings from a lawn with a sizable population of weeds such as dandelion, crabgrass, or plantain or grass that's gone to seed — unless you want to spread the weeds. And don't reuse clippings treated with herbicide; it's just not worth the risk.

Green Living Ground Covers

USE. Decorative and functional.

WHAT THEY ARE. These low-growing plants include thyme, oregano, and creeping phlox for sunny areas; pachysandra, sweet woodruff, and ginger for shady areas. Violets and Johnny-jump-ups thrive in all sorts of conditions. Perennial geraniums such as Biokovo and lancastriense form handsome, expanding, semievergreen clumps with beautiful spring-into-summer blossoms and coppery fall foliage.

HOW TO USE THEM. Creeping perennials should be used in places where you don't walk a lot. Just plant in good soil, water, fertilize occasionally, and watch them take off. A few weeds may sprout until the ground cover becomes firmly entrenched. Then these creeping perennials will grow so thick that nothing else will have a chance.

PROS. Excellent appearance. Persistent spreader. Easy to care for and transplant. Self-sustaining.

CONS. High upfront cost.

GROWING MULCH. Living ground covers, once established, are excellent at controlling weeds.

Green Manure (a.k.a. Cover Crops)

USE. Functional.

WHAT IT IS. More and more vegetable gardeners are discovering the benefits of green manure, such as buckwheat, oats, alfalfa, winter rye, and clover. Green manure can be annual or perennial depending on your plant choices. Garden seed catalogs offer a good variety to choose from.

HOW TO USE IT. Sow a green manure after harvesting crops to fill in bare spots. Small fruit growers who plan in advance may use cover crops. The cover crop remains in the garden over the winter and is tilled under the following spring.

PROS. Besides keeping weeds at bay, green manure decomposes to add nutrients to the soil. Many traditional cover crops also encourage beneficial insects.

Hay

USE. Functional.

WHAT IT IS. Hay probably has been used longer than any other mulching material. Chopped hay is less unsightly than loose hay. First-cut hay is normally hay that has been allowed to go to seed. Second- or third-cut hay often is harvested before it goes to seed, so you might feel a little better about using this on your garden.

HOW TO USE IT. Partially rotted hay makes better mulch than fresh hay. Leave some fresh bales outside through the winter; by spring they will be weathered and damp. Spread 6 to 8 inches (2 to 3 inches if chopped) over garden areas.

PROS. All hay decomposes fairly rapidly and boosts the soil's nitrogen content.

CONS. Fresh hay will steal nitrogen for a short time when it begins to rot.

Leaves

USE. Functional.

WHAT THEY ARE. Besides the basic nutrients that all plants need — nitrogen, phosphorus, and potassium — leaves contain many essential trace mineral elements that the long, penetrating tree roots have retrieved from the deep subsoil.

HOW TO USE THEM. Chop leaves to speed decomposition and prevent soggy matting. Spread 2 to 4 inches of chopped, decomposing leaves on any garden. Alternatively, put down 2 to 3 inches of decaying leaves, then top with 1 or 2 inches of an attractive shredded bark mulch.

....

Pack in the Pachysandra

Pachysandra is inexpensive, spreads slowly but persistently in shady, moist conditions, and is easy to transplant. To begin or expand a patch, find a friend who has plenty and wants to share the bounty. Removing six or eight plants is like taking a bucket of water out of a well — no one will ever notice they are gone. Place the stems and roots where you want the new growth. Cover the roots with soil, then water and keep them somewhat moist until they show small new green leaves.

....

If raking leaves is a dreaded chore, try mowing them with a mower that has a bagging attachment. The mower chops the leaves so you can carry them away in one easy step.

PROS. Look up and down; leaves are all over the place. And they make a splendid mulch in any state of decomposition. Chopped leaves allow water and air to penetrate easily, which lessens the danger of crown rot in some plants.

CONS. Chopped leaves take a bit of extra work. Whole, matted leaves don't let water reach the soil.

Leaf Mold

USE. Functional.

WHAT IT IS. Leaves versus leaf mold? Leaf mold is leaves that have disintegrated to the point where the leaves are no longer distinguishable. Rich leaf mold is exceptionally nutritious for plants.

HOW TO USE IT. Apply like any other organic mulch. Leaf mold mixed into the soil before seed planting can produce a spectacular effect on many plants' growth.

PROS. Leaf mold is chock full of nutrients and microbes ready to nurture any plants you decide to treat with this incredible gift of nature.

Pine Needles

USE. Functional.

WHAT THEY ARE. Pine needles, also called pine straw, are widely available for the raking. They are light, clean, weed free, and easy to handle. In the southern United States gardeners can buy baled pine straw.

HOW TO USE THEM. Rake into a mulch layer 4 to 5 inches deep; it will settle to about 2 inches. Pine needles are especially good for mulching small fruits such as strawberries and blueberries. It is traditional to use them around acid-loving plants, but they do not lower the soil pH too much, so you can use them on other plants as well.

PROS. Pine needles absorb little or no moisture, so water trickles easily through them. They can be used more than once because they decompose so slowly.

CONS. There is little worm activity under pine needle mulch.

....

What's That Strange Smell? Sour Mulch

Wood or bark mulch that's been bagged without air holes or stockpiled and unturned for quite a while may turn "sour" or anaerobic. The lack of oxygen produces toxic substances like methanol, acetic acid, and ammonia that can severely damage the plants it surrounds.

How can you tell whether a mulch is bad? Mostly by the smell. A sour mulch won't have that "freshly cut wood" or "earthy" compost smell. It will stink like rotten eggs, ammonia, or vinegar. If your pile has soured, spread it out to the depth of about a foot and let air get into it. Allow it to dry out completely. Turn the pile regularly and never cover it with plastic or any material that doesn't breathe.

....

Straw

USE. Functional.

WHAT IT IS. Ideally, straw should be free of seeds and chopped. Straw from timothy, oats, barley, wheat, and rye is widely available and relatively cheap. It can be used as a summer mulch around vegetables or as winter protection for trees, shrubs, and strawberries. It's frequently used by homeowners who are trying to start a new lawn.

HOW TO USE IT. A layer of chopped straw needs to be only about 1½ inches thick. Loose straw can be as much as 6 to 8 inches thick, but it does not give a very tidy appearance. In either case, unless the straw is well weathered, add some high-nitrogen fertilizer to the soil before mulching.

CONS. Straw can be a fire hazard. Also, it's not unusual to find little creatures, like mice and voles, setting up camp in a deep straw mulch. If you do use straw, don't lay it right up against the base of your plants.

PAPER MULCHES

PAPER DECAYS EASILY, and as mulch it can come in many forms: from the common newspaper recycled for the garden to commercial mulch paper.

Biodegradable Black Paper

USE. Functional.

WHAT IT IS. This product comes in different widths and may have a line of planting holes cut down the center of the roll.

Municipal Composts

Many municipalities have yard waste collection sites to help alleviate the crisis of limited landfill space. You may be able to get your hands on large amounts of mulching material. Be careful about using it. Many cities and towns simply make big piles of leaves, grass clippings, and whatever else they collect and don't have the equipment to turn and monitor the pile adequately. This could result in sour mulch (see What's That Strange Smell? on page 31). Material may also be contaminated with pesticides; for example, grass clippings from lawns may have been treated with weed killer.

HOW TO USE IT. Place plants in precut holes. It seems to work in much the same way as black polyethylene and is certainly no more difficult to hold in place than plastic.

PROS. It stays intact throughout the growing season.

CONS. It may not decompose on its own as readily as the manufacturer indicates. A light once-over with a rototiller will pulverize it. It is not advertised as having any particular fertilizer value.

Newspaper

USE. Functional.

WHAT IT IS. Mulching with shredded waste paper offers a great opportunity to recycle those stacks of newspapers that are gathering dust in your basement.

HOW TO USE IT. Try shredding newspaper with your lawn mower. It may not be particularly attractive, but it looks better than newspaper laid in folded sheets between rows of plants. Once chopped, newspaper is also more permeable to water. Newspaper mulch can be covered with bark or wood chips to hide it and keep it in place.

PROS. Inexpensive and environmentally friendly.

CONS. Not particularly attractive and may blow around unless secured in place.

NEWSPAPER ON THE GROUND. Cover newspaper mulch with an organic mulch to hold it in place and give the garden a neater appearance.

INORGANIC MULCHES

THE FOLLOWING MULCHES — which include geotextiles, plastic mulch, and stone — are inorganic, so they're not going to add anything to your soil. Some of these mulches might be just the right choice, though, for conserving water, warming the soil, and performing serious weed prevention.

Geotextiles

USE. Functional.

WHAT THEY ARE. Geotextiles are like fabric, only they're made from synthetic fibers that have been woven, knitted, or matted together. Most geotextiles are made from polypropylene, a petroleum by-product. Geotextiles are generally used for weed and erosion control on landscape construction sites.

Geotextiles are available in quantities and sizes appropriate for gardens of all kinds. They also come as specially designed mats for use around trees, shrubs, and difficult planting spots. Geotextiles are very useful for larger planting areas, walkways, patios, and areas where plants are permanently placed.

HOW TO USE THEM. Clear the area of all weeds first. Then there are two options. If you have precut mats or sheets, just lay the mats down and put plants in the holes. If you're working with loose fabric, roll it out and secure the edges with wire prongs or cover with 1 to 3 inches of organic mulch or stone. Some manufacturers recommend planting first, then laying down the fabric between the rows. Others say to put the cloth down and make slits or Xs where your plants will go. You can decide based on your situation.

Covering geotextiles with mulch not only looks good, but it also helps the fabric last longer because the mulch protects it against UV damage and weather exposure.

GEOTEXTILE MULCH. One way to use landscape fabrics is to lay the fabric first, hold it in place with wire prongs, and put plants in place through slits cut in the fabric. Then cover the fabric with an organic mulch.

PROS. Geotextiles have spaces that allow air and water to pass through. Their dark color blocks light needed for weed germination and growth. Most are treated to be UV resistant.

CONS. They don't contribute anything to the soil. Weeds will still grow in the upper layer of mulch that covers a geotextile. Pull up these weeds regularly to keep them from growing into the fabric and creating new holes for other weeds. It's a good idea to turn cover mulch occasionally to disturb other aspiring seedlings.

Plastic (Polyethylene)

USE. Functional.

WHAT IT IS. Plastic mulch from polyethylene has spawned an agricultural approach called plasticulture. Plasticulture uses plastic mulches (as well as drip irrigation, row covers, high and low poly tunnels) for earlier and more bountiful vegetable crops.

Plastic mulch is identified by color (e.g., black, red, and clear) and by type (e.g., infrared transmitting [IRT] mulch and selective reflecting mulch [SRM]).

Black plastic mulch is most commonly used in vegetable production and vegetable gardens. Because no light penetrates its opaque surface, no weeds can grow beneath it. Black plastic mulch reduces soil water loss, increases soil temperature, and improves vegetable yield. Embossed black plastic film has a diamond-shaped pattern to keep the mulch fitted tightly to the bed. Air pockets act as insulation, reducing heat transfer.

Clear plastic mulch allows soil to warm more than colored plastic does, so it's generally used in the cooler regions of the United States, such as New England. Weeds grow under clear mulch, so they must be controlled another way.

Infrared transmitting (IRT) mulch warms the soil like clear plastic does but provides the weed control properties of black mulch. IRT mulch is available in brown or blue-green.

Red plastic mulch is selective reflecting mulch (SRM-Red), a material that performs like black mulch. It warms the soil, controls weeds, and conserves moisture. Red mulch reflects red light up into plants, triggering a vigorous growth response in some vegetables, such as tomatoes and eggplant.

Other colors available include blue, yellow, gray, silver, and orange. Each color reflects light differently, which affects plant growth and development in different ways.

Photo- and biodegradable plastic mulches are also available. They are like black, brown, or clear plastic film mulches but are designed to break down over several months so that they don't have to be removed later.

Plastic mulch is used mainly to get the earliest crop possible and to prevent water evaporation from the soil. It is effective for warm weather crops and transplants: tomato, pepper, eggplant, okra, muskmelon, watermelon, slicing cucumber, summer squash, and sweet corn. It also works for broccoli, cauliflower, pumpkin, and winter squash as transplants.

HOW TO USE IT. Plastic mulches come in rolls 3 to 5 feet wide. There are two mulching methods: Lay plastic over the soil bed between the plant rows or lay it over the entire bed and cut holes in it to place plants. To be most effective, plastic mulch must be in contact with the soil.

Remove all weeds before mulching. It's also best to water the area well before applying the plastic, although walking on wet soil compacts it.

PROS. Plastic mulch has been shown to produce earlier and higher-yielding crops, conserve water, warm the soil, reduce erosion, and reduce weeds. Some types of plastic mulch control insect pests; for instance, silver-surfaced plastic repels some aphids and other flying insect pests.

Plastic of any color practically eliminates moisture evaporation. Water condenses on the underside and drips back into the soil.

CONS. Because it prevents moisture evaporation, plastic also prevents water from penetrating. You will have to take special care to water your plants. Some people install soaker hoses under the mulch.

Plastic mulch doesn't allow the soil to breathe, which can lead to some serious disease problems in ornamental plantings. Tree and shrub roots may suffer from the lack of oxygen.

HOW TO LAY BLACK PLASTIC MULCH

1. Lay the plastic before you plant, making sure the soil is fairly moist.

2. Cut round, X-shaped, or T-shaped holes in the film for plants to grow through and for water to go down.

3. Plant through the holes in the plastic and water seedlings well.

Stone

USES. Decorative and functional.

WHAT IT IS. Stone includes gravel, shale, crushed marble or limestone, even volcanic rocks and flagstones. It is one of the most decorative mulches. Stone is used mostly for ornamental landscape beds and to frame around trees and shrubs. It can be effective and striking in a well-tended rose garden.

HOW TO USE IT. As with all mulches, keep stone from touching the plant stem. Its weight and sharp edges can damage a tender stem, as well as a heavy tree trunk and any extruding roots.

PROS. Stone retains heat from the sun, so it will warm the soil under it well into a cool evening. It's water permeable.

Stone is available in all sorts of textures and colors. It is permanent and low maintenance in ornamental beds. A few trace elements might leach out of a stone mulch over a period of years, but unless you use limestone, it probably won't dissolve noticeably in your lifetime. If you do use limestone chips, keep in mind that these will raise soil pH and should not be spread around acid-loving plants.

Stone mulches clearly won't be blown around by the wind, mat down in the rain, or tie up soil nitrogen.

CONS. Stone isn't cheap. It is heavy to transport and exhausting to apply; consider hiring a contractor to do the hard work. Weeds find their way through crushed stone pretty easily unless the stone is underlaid with geotextiles or plastic.

Stone is highly impractical for the vegetable gardener. Use it where you are sure you will not till.

Because stone is a permanent, low-maintenance mulch, perhaps the most important concern is in picking up a stray stone with the lawn mower and shooting it through the air. For safety's sake rake the grass near the flowerbed occasionally and put any stones back where they belong.

HOW TO CHOOSE A MULCH

WHILE THERE IS NO ONE PERFECT mulch, there are factors that make one mulch a better choice for a given situation. Specific mulches have particular advantages and disadvantages. How do you narrow the list? Here are some general guidelines to help you make the best choice.

Cost

Unless you are looking for something terribly exotic, mulch need not be expensive. There is no reason to mortgage the house or skimp on your plant selections to afford the mulch you've always dreamed of. Mulching is important but not that important. Shop around a little, and price a few types before you decide.

Availability

The availability of a mulch often determines the cost. The laws of supply and demand apply to everything, including mulch. What is plentiful and available is probably cheap — in some instances even free. Check with local municipalities, utility companies, and lumberyards. Many will give away composted leaves or wood chips to someone willing to cart them away. Perhaps a processing plant nearby has excess buckwheat hulls or nut shells. It pays to check with one or two garden clubs in your area. They often have excellent sources for locating mulching materials.

Ease of Application

If you plan to mulch on a large scale, you may be in for a fair amount of initial work. On the other hand, you don't want to be a slave to mulching. For an established bed full of trees and shrubs, you probably won't want to slit dozens of holes in landscape fabric or black plastic to cover it. You also might not want to wrestle with the weight and bulk of crushed stone to mulch a small garden path. Pick a mulch you can handle without having to recruit all the kids from the neighborhood to help you haul it around.

Appearance

Get a peek at what you're thinking of buying, then visualize how it is going to look in your garden. Will those bright red lava rocks go with the rest of the colors in your garden? Black plastic and straw are popular in vegetable gardens but may not look attractive in the peony bed. Eye appeal is a highly personal consideration but definitely worth thinking about.

Water Retention/Penetration

Certainly, you'll want the rainwater to soak down to your plant roots, but permeability isn't as important when you're mulching a pathway. Assess your situation, and choose accordingly. The same is true with air exchange. Plastics won't let air in or out, so they can suffocate plants. If, however, your primary concern is weed control, maybe that's acceptable.

Lasting Qualities

In a vegetable garden you usually turn the mulch into the ground at the end of the season. Chances are you'll want to pick a mulch that decomposes quickly. Conversely, mineral mulches, like gravel and crushed stone, will last for an incredibly long

....

Specialty and Regional Organic Mulches

Depending on where you live, these mulches may not be easy to find. It might be worth the effort to get them, though, when you have the only garden beds on your block covered with fragrant cocoa hulls or attractive crushed oyster shells:

- Buckwheat, cocoa, cotton-seed, peanut, rice hulls
- Cranberry vines
- Eucalyptus wood and bark
- Ground corncobs
- Hops
- Licorice root
- Melaleuca wood and bark mulch
- Oyster shells
- Salt hay, seaweed (kelp)
- Sugarcane
- Walnut shells
- Peanut shells

....

time with a minimal amount of bother. Remember, fine or chopped mulches rot faster, while coarser mulches tend to hang around longer and demand less maintenance.

Chances are you don't want to spend every Saturday afternoon chasing mulch around the yard. If you live on a windy hill, a lightweight mulch such as straw will be an unsatisfactory choice. Paper or plastic mulches need to be anchored with pegs, stones, or something else. And small, fine bark chips can wash away with the first heavy rainfall on even the slightest incline.

PART THREE

HERE'S HOW TO MULCH

In addition to knowing what to use as mulch, the savvy gardener learns how much, where, and when to mulch. Specific recommendations for mulching ornamental plants, vegetables, and fruits follow a little later in this book. For now let's start with some general tips for getting the most out of your mulch.

Keep this mulching primer handy. Whether you are laying plastic for the first time or refreshing last season's wood chips, the following considerations will help you successfully plan and carry out your mulching strategy.

MULCHING 101

Don't try to stretch your mulch too far. Using too little mulch is like trying to paint with a dry brush. The end result isn't worth much. Try to figure out beforehand how much mulch you are going to need. A 100-square-foot garden will need 1¼ to 1½ cubic yards of shredded bark, leaf mold, or gravel to make a mulch layer 4 inches deep. That's eight to nine wheelbarrows full of mulch. It's always good to have extra mulch on hand to replace any that's washed away or decayed, or to cover a newly spaded area. Almost invariably you will end up using more mulch than you thought you would. And you can always stockpile what you do not use.

The thickness of your mulch depends on the material you use. Usually the finer the material, the thinner the mulch layer. Mulch depth can vary from 1 inch for small particles like sawdust to 12 inches for bulky stuff like coarse straw.

Remember that plant roots need to breathe. Air is one of the vital elements in any good soil structure: 50 percent air and 50 percent solid material is a healthy mix. Soil that is too compact has little or no air. One benefit of mulching is that it prevents soil compaction.

Don't mulch so deeply that you suffocate your plants' roots under too much material. Let your soil breathe. A thick mat of wet leaves that bond together and cake can be impenetrable. Fine mulches, unless they are applied sparingly, can compact and prevent air penetration, too.

Replace old mulch that's become decayed and compacted. Mulching promotes shallow root growth. Because the soil stays relatively moist beneath mulch, roots do not have to grow deep and work hard. They can stay near the surface. This means that once you start mulching, you are committed to maintaining it. If you change your mind and remove the mulch in midsummer, your plants may quickly turn crispy and die from lack of water.

Fluff mulch once in a while so it doesn't get too packed down. Break up the dry crust so water can filter through. If your mulch starts sprouting — perhaps because you have used oat straw or hay with lots of seeds — flip the mulch upside down on top of the unwanted seedlings to choke them off.

Choices, Choices, Choices

Refresh or renew mulches in ornamental beds and around shrubs and trees. Using the same type of mulch in these plantings every season is fine, especially because you'll probably just

Mulching Basics

- *Use material that won't compress and smother the soil.*

- *Apply 2 to 4 inches over the root zone.*

- *Never allow any mulch to contact the plant stem.*

need to refresh what's already there. To perk up tired-looking decorative mulch, sometimes just raking will bring larger, more colorful material to the surface. If that isn't enough, you can add new mulch. Remember to remove as much as you replace. For most mulches keep the mulch layer 2 to 4 inches deep, and no thicker. Heaping new mulch on old isn't a problem in itself. Rather, the danger is in overmulching — increasing 3 inches of wood chips to a 6-inch layer, for example. More is not better. Overmulching is likely to kill your plants, maybe not overnight but after a season or two.

Don't use the same mulch year after year in your vegetable garden. This advice is based on the same principle that it is not a good idea to plant the same crop in the same place year in and year out. A good mulching may last for several seasons. When finally it does decompose, it should be replaced by a different material.

Apply thicker mulches to sandy, gravelly soils and thinner mulches to heavy clay soil. Avoid mulching at all in low-lying spots — places that are sometimes likely to be "drowned" with water. Although it isn't always necessary, you can remove mulch during a particularly rainy period to prevent the soil from becoming waterlogged.

Choose the right mulch color for where you live and the plants you're mulching. Darker mulches like buckwheat hulls and walnut shells absorb heat and warm the soil beneath them. Lighter mulches, such as ground corncobs, reflect light and heat the soil less.

It's in the Application

Cultivate around your plants before applying mulch. This is important if your plants have been in the ground awhile without mulch. Loosening the surrounding soil and removing any weeds at this stage will pay off later. Be sure to water the plants generously. Spray with kelp solution or spread fertilizer on the soil, too. After you have prepared the ground, top it with the mulch layer.

After-the-fact mulching cannot do much good if the ground is dried and baked hard. This little bit of advance mulching preparation shouldn't be too much of a chore. Keep in mind that once the mulch is in place you won't have to do any more of this type of work for the rest of the season.

Wait to apply your first mulch until after plants started from seed are established. Mulch between the rows first, not right on top of where the seeds were planted. You can begin to mulch the seedlings just as soon as they are an inch or two higher than the thickness of the mulch. Leave an unmulched area about 6 inches in diameter around each plant for about two weeks. Later, when the mulch is good and dry, bring it within 2 or 3 inches of the stems.

Heavy mulch is most effective if applied when the ground is moist. If the ground is too dry to start with, it will tend to stay dry for the rest of the summer unless there is a real cloudburst.

Do not apply wet mulches, like new grass clippings, on very hot days. When the temperature is above 90°F, such mulches, when wet, tend to generate so much heat that they actually can kill the plants they touch.

Peel off "books" or "flakes" of straw and place them between rows of vegetable plants. This will make a clean path for you to walk on during rainy days and will keep the weeds down. If any weeds come through in force, add more layers.

MULCHING WITH STRAW. Place thick layers from straw bales between rows in the vegetable garden to keep weeds under control and to keep plants clean.

Three Cheers for Microbes and Worms

Bacteria and earthworms are strong allies for any gardener. Without help from lots of microbes in the ground, mulch would never decompose, and the vital elements that are tied up in organic matter would never be released. Worms predigest matter in the soil and liberate chemicals in their castings that plants can use for nourishment. Worms are also excellent indicators of how useful a material will be as mulch, since their presence and activity depend on moderate soil moisture and temperature conditions.

Earthworms are affected by changes in season and temperature. Earthworms are least active during the hottest months and the coldest months. In the summer they can be coaxed into working harder if you keep enough mulch on the garden to keep the soil moist and cool. In the late fall earthworms need to be protected from sudden freezing. Mulching will help protect against rapid temperature changes in the soil.

Troubleshooting with Organic Mulches

Be alert for signs of nitrogen deficiency when you use some organic mulches, such as fresh sawdust or wood chips. Bacteria that break down the mulch and turn it into humus require a large amount of nitrogen themselves, so they take nitrogen from the source most available to them: the soil. This may make plants look yellow and stunted because they are not getting enough nitrogen. Apply your regular fertilizer as directed. Water well.

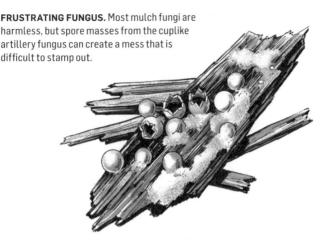

FRUSTRATING FUNGUS. Most mulch fungi are harmless, but spore masses from the cuplike artillery fungus can create a mess that is difficult to stamp out.

Mold can develop in too moist or shaded organic mulch material. To get rid of mold, turn the mulch regularly. Mold does little harm. It seems to offend the human eye more than it bothers soil or plants.

Mulches are excellent places for disease spores to overwinter and multiply. Remove and dispose of mulching material that you know has become disease infested. Don't till it into the soil.

Troubleshooting with Plastic Mulch

Disguise plastic mulch by covering it. If you recognize the advantages of plastic mulch but are offended by the sight of it in your garden, cover the plastic under a thin layer of something else, like pine needles, crushed stone, wood chips, or hulls of some kind.

Apply water-soluble fertilizer through slits in the plastic. If plants under a plastic mulch show signs of needing fertilizer, simply dissolve fertilizer in irrigation water and run it through slits cut into the plastic.

What's Growing in My Wood Mulch?

Wood and bark landscape mulches can be hosts to several fungi that may look strange but are harmless. Many fungi break down wood and bark into material that plants thrive on.

On the other hand, the artillery fungus is a real nuisance along the East Coast. It is so small that it's easy to miss at first. Look closely and you'll see what resemble tiny cream or orange-brown cups holding wee black eggs.

Trouble comes when the fungi reproduce. When light, heat, and moisture conditions are just right, they actually shoot these black eggs (sticky spore masses) at light-colored surfaces, such as a white house or bright car. The "egg" is like a speck of tar. The sticky spore masses are very difficult to remove without damaging the surface of the house or car. One or two spots aren't so noticeable, but en masse they are an unsightly mess. Even if you get them off, the remaining stain requires repainting.

To reduce the likelihood of artillery fungus problems, rake mulch to disturb the fungus and dry out the mulch. Periodically top off decaying mulch with fresh mulch composed of at least 85 percent bark; or replace wood-based mulch with other types, such as black plastic or stone, in areas adjacent to buildings and parking areas.

MULCHING ORNAMENTALS

ORNAMENTAL PLANTS GIVE BEAUTY to our landscapes. They are the trees, shrubs, perennials, annuals, and bulbs placed and cultivated for their visual appeal around our homes and businesses. Every year homeowners spend millions of dollars to add height, variety, texture, and color to their front and backyards. Mulching is a simple way to help protect and enhance that investment.

Mulching is an integral part of landscaping for several reasons. A richly textured, attractive mulch adds a professional touch to any ornamental bed. Mulching an ornamental bed conserves water, controls weeds, mediates soil temperature, and stops erosion. Healthy ornamentals improve a property's value, and they give you more enjoyment of your time at home.

Because most landscape plantings are perennial in nature, you can use more permanent mulching techniques and materials. It's worth the time and effort to lay down a landscape fabric and cover it with stones if you don't plan to remove it in the fall.

Mulch for landscaping, be it for a single tree or a handsome mixed bed of perennials, shrubs, and annuals, should appeal to the eye. Decorative mulches include shredded barks, stones, wood chips, and cocoa hulls. Ground covers such as thyme and pachysandra can act as excellent living mulch, keeping weeds at bay and soil in place in difficult or large areas.

Geotextile fabric topped with shredded bark, natural or colored wood chips, or stone is a popular landscape mulch. Redwood chips placed over landscape fabric is a good way to add color.

The basics of mulching apply to ornamental use, just as they do for vegetable gardens. Choose your mulch thoughtfully. Before applying any mulch, water the ground well and remove all weeds. Fertilize your plants according to package directions. Apply mulch evenly as if it were a blanket, 2 to 4 inches deep, depending on your mulch and the soil conditions. Don't place mulch against any living stems, trunks, or branches.

To refresh old mulch, give it a light raking to fluff it up, renew the color, and break through any crust. If that doesn't do the trick, remove an inch or two of the organic mulch (wood chips, bark). Then top with new mulch, adding about as much as you removed. Keep the depth of the mulch in the 2 to 4 inch range. With mulch, more is not always better. Overmulching can be fatal to the plants you are trying to help.

Trees

Probably the number one cause of death for newly planted trees and shrubs is the lack of adequate water. We already know that mulch can help solve that problem. Mulching around the tree base also reduces the incidence of lawn mower damage, another cause of tree death. A good covering of mulch, 3 to 4 inches deep, right after planting will go a long way toward protecting the base of your trees. Before mulching a new transplant, clear away weeds and grasses from the soil surrounding the trunk. A circle 3 to 5 feet wide is a good start. Water generously. Then mulch that cleared area to suppress weeds and grass. This boundary will also help you resist the urge to mow right up to the trunk of the tree.

ESTABLISHED TREE MULCHING. Mulch an area at least as large as a tree's dripline to reduce weed competition for water and nutrients needed by the tree.

For mulching under established trees, clear weeds and grasses to the tree's dripline, which is the shady area beneath the tree's canopy. If that's too overwhelming an area, clear as large an area as you can. Something is better than nothing.

Next, apply organic fertilizer as directed, then water the area well. Top with 3 to 4 inches of organic mulch.

A work-saving alternative when temperatures drop in the fall is to spread fresh wood chips out to the dripline. They'll do double duty. The heat from their decay will kill grass under the tree canopy and the chips will act as mulch, too.

Organic mulches like wood chips, shredded bark or nuggets, cocoa hulls, pine needles, leaf mold, and shredded leaves are all smart choices for mulching trees. These mulches decompose, adding to the soil nutrients that are easily depleted by all the tree's shallow feeder roots. Crushed stone and gravel are fine, but they won't enrich the soil. Be careful when applying any rock-type mulches around woody plants. Rock mulches can do serious damage to woody plants if they jab into the base of the tree. Remember to keep all types of mulch at least 6 inches from the tree trunk.

Shrubs

To mulch shrubs, follow the basic mulching guidelines (see Mulching Basics box on page 49). Remove as many weeds and grass clumps as possible, especially in the shady area under the shrub's branches. Apply fertilizer if needed, according to package directions. Water well. Then apply your mulch of choice in an even 2- to 4-inch blanket over the root area. Remember,

Hold the Volcanoes!

Don't succumb to the common practice of building a volcano of mulch up around a tree or shrub. If you do, you might as well say last rites for your plant. Dark, moist mulch right against bark is the perfect place for insects, diseases, rot, and gnawing critters to feast.

Think "blanket of mulch" instead. Start mulch at least 6 inches from the tree trunk or shrub base. Apply an even layer, 2 to 4 inches deep, over the entire area beneath a tree or shrub. Doing this will smother weeds and allow water to seep evenly into the soil.

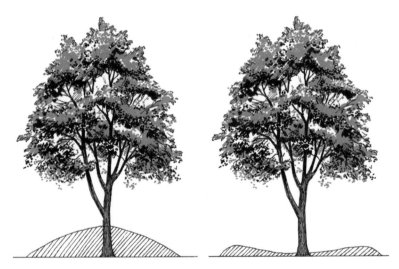

NO VOLCANO MULCHING. A mulch volcano (left) can lead to problems. Proper mulching (right) leaves space around the base of a tree.

an organic mulch such as leaf mold or shredded bark will feed your plants for many months to come. Avoid placing mulch in direct contact with the shrub's base and branches.

Mixed Beds: Perennials and/or Annuals

New beds. Mulching a new mixed bed of perennials and annuals is easy. Put in the plants. Water generously, and fertilize as needed. Carefully shovel mulch around the new transplants, making sure not to allow mulch to rest against the stems or on the crowns. Mulch on crowns and against stems invites rot, disease, and insect damage. Spread the mulch until you get an even blanket of material that is 3 to 4 inches deep.

If your plants are small, such as young annuals, 2 inches of mulch is fine. If you've grouped annuals close together, don't sprinkle mulch between the flowers. Just start mulching an inch or two outside the group. Remember that one of your major interests for mulching is weed control, meaning that a deeper mulch layer is best where weeds might be tempted to take root.

Keep a close eye on your mixed bed for a week or two. If your plants start to turn brown or look wilted, check to make sure mulch isn't in direct contact with them. If it is, pull away the mulch. As a reminder, mulch is harmful when placed too close to stem and leaves. It can stifle airflow, trap moisture, and become home to insects and diseases.

Established beds. Mulching an established mixed perennial bed is best done in spring after the soil has warmed. At this time the plants will be filling out and you should be able to move easily through the garden. Some perennials are slow to emerge, so walk (and mulch) carefully. Also watch for sprouting seeds; they may be developing into more perennials you'll want to move or cultivate in place.

If you've planted in clusters or groups, mulch outside the clusters and cultivate inside. You want your perennials to have as much room to fill in as possible. The ultimate goal is to have a perennial bed full of, well, blooming perennials! Every year your perennials should spread farther and wider so you'll need less and less mulch.

Weed, water well, and fertilize as needed before mulching. If mulch from the last season remains, hoe to loosen it before topping off with a new batch.

If you just don't get to mulching early on in the spring season, don't worry. Anytime is better than no time. Just remember to weed and water well in preparation for mulching. Then

For the Best of All Mulch Worlds

For an attractive landscape that saves money and gives your plants the most nutrition, try a two-layer approach to mulching ornamentals. It'll look great immediately, and even better next season after the leaf mold has fed your plants.

1. Apply 1 to 2 inches of leaf mold or chopped leaves.

2. Top with 1 to 2 inches of shredded bark.

allow the foliage to dry before shoveling on the mulch. Be sure to keep the mulch an inch or two away from the base of each perennial to avoid causing rot to their crowns and stems. Otherwise, mulch in their crowns and against stems is likely to cause rot.

Winter Mulch

Generally, if you mulched in the spring, then you do not necessarily need to mulch in the winter. For fall transplants (shrubs and perennials) and late-season divisions, though, a loose winter mulch of evergreen boughs, pine needles, or pine bark chips provide excellent extra protection. The same is true for marginally hardy plants and temperamental shrubs. Use a light mulch that won't mat down, resist water, or make too comfortable a home for rodents. Whole leaves, although handy, aren't

---

Rhododendrons and Azaleas

Both rhododendrons and azaleas prefer acidic soils, and your mulch selection can play a part in helping them get the soil type they want. Choose an organic mulch, such as shredded leaves or pine needles. A dry mulch of shredded leaves, spread 10 to 12 inches deep, can be laid down at planting (these will decompose quickly to give you a 3- or 4-inch layer). A 2- or 3-inch layer of pine needles will also do the trick, as will wood chips, if sufficiently weathered. Mulching helps cool the plants' shallow roots during the summer and will retain soil moisture year-round for these mostly evergreen plants.

---

a good idea because they will clump, mat, keep water out, and suffocate anything below. Shredded leaves work well, though. Remember to remove the light mulch in spring when you see new sprouts. Keep some boughs on hand in case you need to cover plants quickly as protection from a late frost.

Roses

Rose mulching offers a shining example of the differences between summer and winter mulches. Summer mulching is done in the spring to control weeds and maintain soil moisture. Winter mulches, put down after the ground has started to cool in the fall, serve to protect the plant from temperature extremes and soil heaving.

Winter mulching for roses. Here are three methods for mulching roses in winter. Whichever system you select, water the soil well before covering your roses and remove the mulch in the spring before new growth begins. If the winter mulch is left on until the buds start swelling, the new growth may be put into shock when you uncover it.

MOUNDED SOIL/MULCH METHOD

Take soil or organic mulch from elsewhere in the garden and make a mound of 10 to 12 inches around the base of the rose bush. Do this after the first hard frost. If you do this too early, the roses may be fooled into a late growth spurt, which will delay dormancy and lead to more, not less, winter injury.

MOUNDED SOIL. For mulching roses in winter, mound soil/mulch at least 10 inches around each bush.

ROSE CONE/SYNTHETIC FIBER BLANKET METHOD

In areas where the temperature stays well below freezing for most of the season, you will need to provide some additional protection. Some growers lean toward the Styrofoam rose cones that fit around the mounds; others prefer ground corncobs, sawdust, or chopped leaves. Synthetic fiber blankets are an attractive winter protection. However, rose cones can cause overheating during those warm, sunny January thaws. To help keep your roses from "frying," poke a ventilation hole in the top.

ROSE CONE. To keep a lightweight rose cone in place, weigh down the cone with a brick.

WIRE CAGE METHOD

Wire cages filled with leaves or compost are often used instead of the Styrofoam cones. These cages needn't be stuffed to the gills with leaves. An overstuffed cage makes for poor air circulation that may lead to disease.

WIRED CAGE. A cylinder of wire mesh holds mounded soil in place around rose canes.

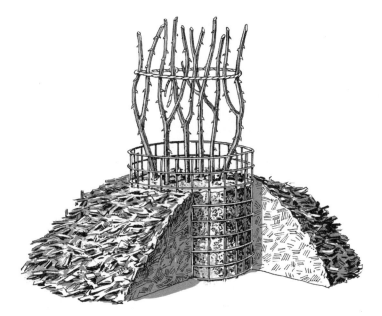

Summer mulching roses. Mulching roses during the growing season prevents damage to shallow roots during cultivation. Be careful not to mulch right up to the base of rose bushes, and do not overwater the beds. Moist, damp conditions can foster many rose diseases.

Bulbs

Mulching hardy bulbs is not essential. But in a cold-winter area the insulating value of a thick organic mulch can't be overlooked. Two to 4 inches of shredded leaves, bark nuggets, wood chips, corncobs — just about any mulch that doesn't pack down — is fine for bulbs. Apply mulch after the ground is frozen. Remove the mulch in the early spring at the first sign of green sprouts.

....

Some Good Mulches for Roses

Shredded bark, fine bark nuggets, cocoa hulls, or buckwheat hulls are perfect summer mulches for showcasing expensive specimen roses. This is one instance where the added cost of these mulches might be justified. The dark, rich colors associated with these types of mulch can really accent an already impressive rose display.

Decorative, organic mulches are also excellent for the easy-care rose varieties. If you fertilize and water well before applying mulch to ever-blooming Carefree Wonder roses, for example, there's little else to do for the season but water occasionally, relax, and admire the blossoms.

....

MULCHING VEGETABLES

MANY ANNUAL AND PERENNIAL VEGETABLES benefit from mulching during the year. Following is a list of commonly grown vegetables accompanied by recommendations of how and when they might need mulch. While considering the

TWO-STEP MULCHING

When seeds are first planted, mulch between rows.

When plants are established, move mulch closer to plants.

suggestions made here, keep several things in mind: (1) the general mulching guidelines offered earlier in this book (see Mulching Basics box on page 49), (2) your own experience with a particular vegetable, (3) the climate in your area, and (4) the idiosyncrasies of your garden, such as the soil condition, drainage, the amount of sunlight, and the types of pests.

Asparagus

If you are just starting a new asparagus bed, mulching probably is not necessary until the second spring. However, if you live in a cold place, you will want to mulch for winter protection even in the first year. Hay, leaves, and straw are just a few mulches that are excellent for winter protection of asparagus.

In the spring there is no need to remove winter mulch. The tips will come right up through the mulch whenever they are ready. Eight inches of hay mulch is not too much for asparagus. The primary function of this mulch is weed control, but it may have other fringe benefits.

To extend your asparagus season, divide your bed into two parts in the spring. Mulch half of the bed heavily with a fine material such as chopped leaves or leaf mold. Leave the other half unmulched until the shoots begin to break through the mulched half. Then mulch where you did not mulch before. This technique should extend the asparagus season, because the part of the bed that got its start without mulch will begin to bear one or two weeks earlier than the part that started out with mulch. Don't worry about weed control with the temporarily unmulched bed — those first asparagus shoots will poke

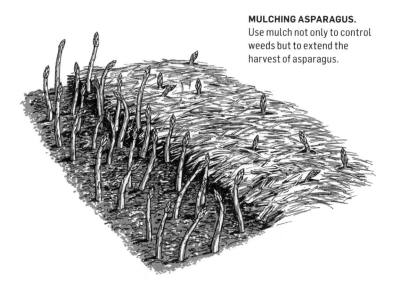

MULCHING ASPARAGUS.
Use mulch not only to control weeds but to extend the harvest of asparagus.

through early in the season, long before any weeds take hold. If you are prompt with your second application of mulch, you'll still have excellent weed control.

Beans

You can mulch beans two or three weeks after planting. Mulching is especially beneficial to beans because it inhibits weed growth. The finer the mulch the better, particularly if you like to plant beans in wide rows. Bean roots grow close to the surface, meaning that any deep or extensive cultivation to halt weeds will also result in undesirable root pruning of the beans themselves.

Beets, Rutabaga, and Turnips

Beets prefer a nonacidic soil, so it is probably better not to mulch them with pine needles exclusively. You can use just about anything else for mulch. In fact, adding ground limestone or lime to the soil, or mixing it with the mulch, may be a good idea. Ideally, leaves or leaf compost should be spread on beet plots at least once a year, then worked into the soil as fertilizer.

A light mulch of grass clippings can be put down right after planting beet seeds. Doing so will conserve moisture and prevent the sun from baking the soil hard. As soon as the sprouts appear, pull this mulch back a bit for a while because beets are highly susceptible to damping off, which is a fungal disease promoted by damp, stagnant air around seedlings. As the growing season progresses, increase the thickness of the mulch by adding more layers of straw or hay. And after the rows have been thinned, tuck the mulch in close to the maturing plants. This procedure seems to work well for turnips and rutabagas, too.

Broccoli and Cauliflower

Broccoli and cauliflower can be mulched shortly after the plants have been moved outdoors and set in the garden. Any nonacidic organic mulch is fine — it will preserve moisture and discourage some insects. Late in the season the mulch can extend a plant's productive time. Broccoli and cauliflower can stand a maximum of 4 to 6 inches of organic mulch.

Polyethylene plastic works well with broccoli. If you use it, lay the plastic, cut holes, and transplant through the openings. A little fertilizer and lime ahead of time is probably in order.

Cabbage

After your transplants are well established, partially decomposed mulch can be tucked right up under the leaves around your cabbage plants. This may slow their growth somewhat, but they will grow tender, green, and succulent.

Light-reflecting mulch is especially suitable for cabbage. It discourages some disease-carrying aphids.

If you live in a climate that normally experiences mild winters, you might like to plant cabbage seed and cover the beds with a mulch in the late fall — in November or early December. Re-cover the bed with coarser mulch, such as twigs or evergreen boughs, as soon as the seedlings appear. In spring, when you uncover them, you will have some hardy babies for early transplanting.

Cantaloupes and Other Melons

Cantaloupes and other melons need lots of moisture as well as heat, from the time they come up until they are fully grown. Research has shown that larger yields result when green IRT plastic mulch is used where the melons are planted. This type of mulch helps to warm the soil, eliminates weeds, and maintains a more constant supply of water to the roots.

A thick organic mulch is designed to do pretty much the same thing as plastic mulch. Hay, grass clippings, buckwheat hulls, cocoa shells, and newspapers work fine. It probably is better to stay away from sawdust and leaves. The mulch should be in place before the fruit develops, because handling may damage the tender melons. Once the fruit is formed, it will be resting on a clean carpet of mulch and won't be as prone to rot.

Carrots

Mulch should be used sparingly on carrots. When you sow carrots, you might want to spread a very thin mulch, say of grass clippings, over the beds to prevent the soil surface from forming a crust that the sprouting seeds can't break through. Water this mulch if you like, but be careful that the tiny seeds don't wash away. When the slender seedlings come up, be sure that the mulch does not interfere with them.

Have you tried leaving your carrots in the ground during the early winter months to save on storage space in the house? They can be kept in the ground, covered with a heavy mulch to prevent freezing and thawing damage. Once dug up they won't keep long, but you may prefer them to frozen or canned carrots from the supermarket.

Celery

The traditional way to "blanch" celery is with a soil mulch. To do this, pull earth around the plants as they grow higher, until finally, when the celery is fully grown, the celery rows are about 18 inches high and only the green tops are showing. As a cleaner alternative, try an organic mulch rather than soil to blanch your celery. Chopped leaves are best; whole leaves may dry out and blow away.

Celery that is protected with a deep mulch will produce crisp, tender hearts until Thanksgiving or later. Ideally the heavily mulched rows should be covered with plastic, or some other waterproof material to form a tent. With this type of protection, the ground stays dry and will not freeze too hard.

For cleaner plants, blanch celery with mulch, such as chopped leaves or newspaper, instead of soil.

You will be able to dig out celery any time you want it, even in midwinter. Just shovel away some snow, remove the tent, and uncover your desired amount of celery. Celery that is protected this way keeps better than if stored in a root cellar.

Corn

Some gardeners keep a permanent organic mulch on their corn patches. At planting time they just run a straight line with a string and push their corn seeds down through the mulch with their fingers.

Permanent mulchers argue that crows seem to be non-plussed by the heavy layer of mulch over corn. Without this mulch crows often will pull out small corn plants nearly as fast as they show aboveground. They are after the tender, just-sprouted kernels. If the corn has had a chance to get a good head start under mulch, the plants will yield disappointing results to the average crow.

Where soil warmth is a concern in late spring/early summer, hold off on mulching corn seedlings until the plants are about a foot tall. Use any mulch that preserves soil moisture and adds nutrients to give the corn an extra boost.

Cucumbers

Chopped leaves, leaf mold, straw, and old hay are good for mulching cucumbers. These types of mulch can be put around the plants when they are about 3 inches high and before the vines really start to extend. Cucumbers require a lot of moisture, which the mulch will help to retain. Some organic mulches will invite slugs, snails, insects, and diseases to your cukes. To be on the safe side, keep the mulch 3 or 4 inches away from the main plant.

Eggplant

Eggplant needs all the warmth it can get. Red and black plastic mulches have been used successfully to warm soil and increase fruit yield. However, if you are planning to use organic mulch, don't apply it until after the ground has really had a chance to warm up. Also, avoid disturbing the earth immediately around eggplant. Once the soil is warm enough, mulch will smother most weeds before they grow big enough to be pulled.

The roots of these finicky plants prefer to grow and feed in the top 2 inches of soil. If there is too little moisture there, the leaves of eggplant turn yellow, become spotted, and drop off. If there is too much moisture, the plant will not bear fruit. Mulch can help to keep a uniform supply of moisture in the soil.

Garlic

Garlic can be mulched when the plants are 6 to 8 inches high. Use a fine mulch like hulls, grass clippings, or chopped leaves. For more advice see the entry on Onions on page 78.

Kale

Kale is an incredibly hardy vegetable. It can be grown nearly any time of year. A fall or winter crop of kale may be left in the field, covered lightly with something like hay or straw. Later in the winter simply remove the snow (one of the mulches kale seems to like best, by the way) and cut the leaves as you want them. Kale will sometimes keep this way all winter, provided that it doesn't get smothered by ice after a thaw.

Leeks

Leeks and scallions can be mulched lightly with anything from straw to wood shavings. Just be sure that the mulch does not interfere with the very young seedlings. For more advice see the Onions entry below.

Lettuce

Leaf lettuce does well in semishade and in rich soil. A coarse mulch such as twigs, rye straw, or even pine boughs can be used in the seedbed. As the leaves grow, move the mulch right up underneath them. This does four things: It holds the soil moisture, keeps the leaves from being splashed with mud, prevents rot, and maintains the cool root zone that this cold-season vegetable requires for optimum production.

You can apply as much as 3 inches of mulch as soon as head lettuce is 3 or 4 inches high and has started to send out its leaves.

Onions

Onions can and should be mulched during long hot spells. Chopped leaves can be sprinkled among the green shoots even if they are 2 or 3 inches high. Mulched onions will grow more slowly and be more succulent than onions grown without mulch. A little more mulch can be added as the tops develop.

Parsley

In places where winter is not as harsh as northern climates, parsley can be protected by mulch throughout the winter. It can be planted in cold frames in August — or even later — covered with hay, left in the frames all winter, and transplanted to the garden in the early spring. Parsley is susceptible to crown rot, so summer mulches should be kept 5 to 6 inches away from the plant.

Parsnips

Parsnips do not grow well in tight, compacted soil: Instead of growing one straight root, they divide into three or four, which makes the root worthless. Mulching can help here by preventing soil compaction. Note that parsnips prefer a soil with a pH of about 6.5, so don't use an acidic mulch.

Most gardeners can eat parsnips from their gardens all winter if the plants are heaped high with leaves or some other protective mulch as cold weather moves in. Parsnips store very well. Don't harvest them until after the first heavy frost; they won't have reached their peak of quality until then anyway.

Peas

In northern regions gardeners don't have any trouble creating cool and damp conditions for peas without using mulch. It is easy to overdo mulching peas in a cool climate, but the soil around peas does need to be cool and damp for germination and growth.

To grow peas in warmer places, or to grow pea varieties like Wando later in the summer, mulch with a thin layer of grass clippings, straw, or hay when the seeds are sown. As the plants get started, you can increase the mulch to insulate the soil from the atmosphere and the hot sun. Mulching in this way all but ensures a cool, moist root zone.

The last time you pick your peas each season, pull up the whole vine before you remove the pods. This should help save your back. The vines should be stacked and saved, too. Chopped or whole, they are a nitrogen-rich mulch that can be used on the garden, except on other peas (for the same reason you rotate crops — to stave off disease problems).

Peppers

The growing habits of peppers are very much like those of tomatoes. Set transplants out in red or black plastic mulch, or black paper mulch. This mulch will collect the heat of the day and help maintain a warm soil temperature for a while into the night.

Potatoes

Potatoes, if you use mulch, don't even need to be planted! You can lay seed potatoes on soil or on top of the previous year's mulch, then cover them with a 12-inch-thick layer of hay or straw. You can harvest early potatoes from their thick mulch bed, then replace the covering.

MULCHING POTATOES. Harvest new potatoes from under mulch and re-cover plants to allow additional tubers to develop.

Deep mulch also seems to thwart pesky Colorado potato beetles, because it provides an environment conducive to predators of these beetles.

Pumpkins

Pumpkins profit from freshly cut hay, composted leaves, and straw. Mulch around each hill. As the crop starts to mature, use any coarse mulch that keeps the fruit off the ground.

Radishes

Mulch is not recommended for quick-growing plants like radishes, as there usually is not enough time for the mulch to do them any good. For the most part, plants that prefer cool, moist soil respond better to mulches than those plants that revel in hot sun and dry soil.

Rhubarb

Spread a thick mulch of strawy manure over the bed after the ground freezes in the winter. In the spring rake the residue aside to allow the ground to warm and the plants to sprout. Then draw the residue, together with a thick new blanket of straw mulch, up around the plants. Hay, leaves, or sawdust also makes excellent mulch for rhubarb.

Spinach and Swiss Chard

Once the seedlings are well established, spinach and chard can be mulched with grass clippings, chopped hay, straw, or ground corncobs and be better for it. Spinach prefers nonacidic soil, so avoid pine needles and sawdust. In any case, don't put down a summer mulch until the leaves have had a chance to make a good growth.

Squash

Squash can use an extra dose of mulch, especially during hot, dry spells. The mulch, whether it be hay or chopped leaves, can be as deep as 4 inches. Leave the center open so that some heat can get to the middle of the plant. The mulch over the rest of the patch will preserve moisture and discourage some bugs.

Sweet Potatoes

Sweet potatoes are ravenous feeders and are happiest in plenty of moisture. Old leaves and grass clippings make good mulches, as do the old standbys, hay and straw. Consider black plastic as a soil-warming mulch if growing sweet potatoes in northern climes.

Tomatoes

Some vegetables such as tomatoes (as well as peppers and corn) need thoroughly warmed soil to encourage ideal growth. A mulch that is applied too early in the spring, before soil temperatures have had a chance to climb a little in frost-zone areas, will slow such crops.

However, black and red plastic mulches, used in commercial cultivation, are increasingly popular among gardeners who want earlier crops and higher yields. These plastic mulches warm the soil so you can start planting earlier and continue harvesting longer. They also conserve moisture and control weeds. They are best applied either before or soon after plants are in the ground.

If you choose not to use plastic, a good time to mulch with other materials (hay, straw, chopped leaves) is right after the flowers appear. Blossom-end rot can be caused by a variable moisture supply. Mulch keeps a more consistent supply of moisture around the roots of the plants. If you have lots of mulch and few sticks to use as tomato stakes, forget about staking. Let your plants run around freely over the mulch, and let the fruit ripen there.

Watermelon

Here is still another plant that should not be mulched until the soil is really warm — or use black or IRT plastic mulch to warm the soil. Watermelons demand all kinds of soil moisture. The best time to apply organic mulch is when the soil has been dampened thoroughly. Up to 6 inches of mulch can be spread over the entire patch, if you like, to prevent rot and to keep the fruit soil free.

MULCHING PERENNIAL FRUITS

LIKE ANY OTHER CULTIVATED PLANT, fruit trees and berry bushes benefit from mulching. In addition, mulching helps to keep fruit clean and palatable for harvest. Following are recommendations for mulching these fruits in spring, summer, autumn, and winter.

Spring

As the snow starts to melt during those first warm, sunny days of spring, loosen mulch where it has been crushed by snow, if you like, but don't remove it too early. The plants may be frost-heaved out of the ground or begin to grow too soon and get nipped by frost. Spring is a good time to scout around and see what you can scavenge in the way of mulching materials. It also is the time to plow, spade, or rototill winter mulch into seedbeds where you will be planting your annual plants.

Move protective mulch away from plants gradually, and let it lie off to the side, but within easy reach. If possible, remove the final layers of mulch on a cloudy day so that any young shoots that have started are not blasted suddenly by brilliant sunshine. Once the winter mulch is off completely, leave it off for several days, or even a couple of weeks, before you start to mulch again. Give the earth plenty of time to warm up.

In the late spring start mulching again. Your aim is to conserve soil moisture and control weeds before they get a head start. Mulch far enough away from your fruit trees — out at least to the dripline (that's the outer perimeter of the tree if you are looking straight down on it) — to be sure your mulch is directly over the tiny feeder roots.

Summer

Summer is the time when mulching should start to pay dividends. During hot spells, roots should thrive in the weedless, cool, moist ground under the mulch. You need to do nothing except have a look every now and again, and renew the mulch wherever weeds show signs of getting the upper hand. Pull any weeds that show up.

Be crafty about choosing materials for summer mulching. Because your fruits will not be tilled, use organic mulches to encourage earthworms into your perennial beds. Worms will help aerate the soil. A continuous mulch around thick-stemmed shrubs and trees should be a coarse, heavy material that allows plenty of water through but that is not going to decay too rapidly (this mulch should last for several years).

One thing to look out for is crown rot in small fruits — strawberries, for example — during the early summer months.

If there have been especially heavy rains, postpone your mulching until the soil is no longer waterlogged. Do not allow mulches to touch the bases of your plants. The idea here is to permit the soil to stay dry and open to the air around the immediate area of the plant.

Autumn

The longer the perennial's roots can stay at work in the fall, the better — up to a point. Late mulching can prolong a plant's growing season because it provides a buffer zone against frost. Roots will continue to grow in soil as long as moisture is still available there. When the soil water freezes and is unavailable to roots, they stop growing. Increase your mulch volume gradually for a while to insulate the soil and to prevent early freezing of soil moisture.

Once the frost has been on the pumpkin more than a couple of times, your plants probably should be given a hardening-off period that is similar to the one you gave them in the spring. Remove the mulch gradually until the plants are obviously dormant and the ground is frozen.

By now you should be collecting materials for winter mulching. Maybe you will want to cut evergreen boughs. They do a great job of holding snow (which is a superb mulch) in places where it might otherwise be blown away. After harvest time, push mulch back away from fruit trees, leaving an open space around the trunks. If you anticipate that a winter rodent problem will develop, remember that you can wrap wire mesh, hardware cloth, or plastic protectors around tree trunks and berry canes.

Fall is the best time to make use of your chopper to grind up plant residues for future use as mulch. Use your rototiller, if you have one, for tilling in leaves between rows. Till in the summer mulch, too.

Winter

Mulch your annual beds early — before frost really has settled into the soil — so that earthworms and beneficial micro-organisms can stay at work longer during the cold months.

Mulch perennial fruits after the ground is frozen, so that plants cannot be "heaved" out of the ground when the soil expands and contracts on alternately freezing and thawing days. Note that because winter mulch prevents the absorption of heat in the spring, it doesn't allow anything to grow until after the last killing frost has passed. Once the killing frosts have abated for the season, you can finally remove the winter mulch.

FRUIT TREES

Apply organic mulches, such as straw, hay, shredded leaves, grass clippings, or bark, to a depth of 6 inches.

Leave a space of several inches between the mulch and the base of trees to deter rodents; use tree guards if necessary.

STRAWBERRIES

Apply 3 inches of straw or chopped hay after planting, being careful not to cover plant leaves with mulch.

Add another 3 to 5 inches of straw for winter mulching whenever temperatures stay below 20°F for any extended period of time.

When removing mulch in spring, put half of it in the pathways between rows and leave the other half for plants to grow through.

RASPBERRIES AND BLACKBERRIES

Apply 3 or 4 inches of chopped hay, straw, or bark as a permanent mulch to the row, or over the entire soil surface after planting.

Maintain permanent mulch by replenishing annually.

BLUEBERRIES

Spread weathered sawdust, pine needles, or pine bark mulch 3 to 4 inches deep, keeping it away from plant stems.

Maintain permanent mulch by replenishing annually.

CURRANTS AND GOOSEBERRIES

Lay down 2 or 3 inches of an organic mulch, such as straw, leaves, or grass clippings, while planting your bushes. Replenish annually.

INDEX

Page numbers in *italic* indicate illustrations.

OTHER STOREY TITLES YOU WILL ENJOY

The Complete Compost Gardening Guide
by Barbara Pleasant & Deborah L. Martin
With the natural Six-Way Compost Gardening System, you will learn
the ruling principles for successfully improving your garden with healthy
compost. This thorough, informative tour of materials and innovative
techniques helps you turn an average vegetable plot into a rich incubator of
healthy produce and flower beds into vibrant tapestries of bountiful blooms
all season long.
320 pages. Paper. ISBN 978-1-58017-702-3.
Hardcover. ISBN 978-1-58017-703-0.

Let It Rot! **by Stu Campbell**
The book that helped start the composting movement teaches you how to
recycle waste to create soil-nourishing compost, with advice for starting
and maintaining a composting system, building bins, and using compost.
160 pages. Paper. ISBN 978-1-58017-023-9.

The Pruning Answer Book
by Lewis Hill & Penelope O'Sullivan
When should you prune? How much should you remove? What's the
difference between pinching and heading back? How can you be sure that
you're not harming your plants? For all of your pruning questions,
The Pruning Answer Book has the answers. Clear instructions, expert advice,
and detailed illustrations give you everything you need to successfully
prune flowering trees, fruit and nut trees, shrubs, brambles, evergreens,
vines, groundcovers, and more.
384 pages. Flexibind with paper spine. ISBN 978-1-60342-710-4.

These and other books from Storey Publishing are available
wherever quality books are sold or by calling 1-800-441-5700.
Visit us at *www.storey.com* or sign up for our newsletter
at *www.storey.com/signup*.